WE FOUND LOVE AND AN EXQUISITE SET OF PORCELAIN FIGURINES ABOARD THE SS *FARNDALE AVENUE*

by David McGillivray and
Walter Zerlin Jr.

‖SAMUEL FRENCH‖

FOR PRODUCTION ENQUIRIES
United Kingdom and World
excluding North America
licensing@concordtheatricals.co.uk
020-7054-7200
Each title is subject to availability from Concord Theatricals, depending upon country of performance.

The moral right of David McGillivray and Walter Zerlin Jr. to be identified as authors of this work has been asserted in accordance with Section 77 of the Copyright, Designs and Patents Act 1988.

USE OF COPYRIGHTED MUSIC

A licence issued by Concord Theatricals to perform this play does not include permission to use the incidental music specified in this publication. In the United Kingdom: Where the place of performance is already licensed by the PERFORMING RIGHT SOCIETY (PRS) a return of the music used must be made to them. If the place of performance is not so licensed then application should be made to PRS for Music (www.prsformusic.com). A separate and additional licence from PHONOGRAPHIC PERFORMANCE LTD. (www.ppluk.com) may be needed whenever commercial recordings are used. Outside the United Kingdom: Please contact the appropriate music licensing authority in your territory for the rights to any incidental music.

USE OF COPYRIGHTED THIRD-PARTY MATERIALS

Licensees are solely responsible for obtaining formal written permission from copyright owners to use copyrighted third-party materials (e.g., artworks, logos) in the performance of this play and are strongly cautioned to do so. If no such permission is obtained by the licensee, then the licensee must use only original materials that the licensee owns and controls. Licensees are solely responsible and liable for clearances of all third-party copyrighted materials, and shall indemnify the copyright owners of the play(s) and their licensing agent, Concord Theatricals Ltd., against any costs, expenses, losses and liabilities arising from the use of such copyrighted third-party materials by licensees.

IMPORTANT BILLING AND CREDIT REQUIREMENTS

If you have obtained performance rights to this title, please refer to your licensing agreement for important billing and credit requirements.

WE FOUND LOVE AND AN EXQUISITE
SET OF PORCELAIN FIGURINES
ABOARD THE SS *FARNDALE AVENUE*

First produced at the Gardner Centre, Brighton, on 29th
November, 1990, with the following cast of characters:

Mrs Reece	Victoria Plum
(playing Beauregard St Clair;	
Lillian; Steward; Mavis Smith;	
Captain Brown; A Jolly Tar)	
Thelma	Teresa Selfe
(playing Constance Lombard;	
A Jolly Tar)	
Felicity	Debbie Holden
(playing Daisy; Cicely;	
Captain Jones; Porter; A Jolly Tar)	
Gordon	
(playing Noël Nightingale,	Jack Milner
Gwendolyn; A Jolly Tar)	
Disc Jockey	

Directed by David McGillivray

(NB. It is preferable for **Gordon** and the **Disc Jockey** to
be played by different actors)

CHARACTERS

Mrs Reece: elegant, bossy, enterprising; 50s.
Thelma: quick-tempered prima donna; late 40s.
Gordon: long-suffering stage manager, frozen-faced and monotonous when acting; age immaterial.
Felicity: nervous, well-meaning but incompetent actress; late 20s.
Disc Jockey: slick and extrovert performer; late 20s.

SYNOPSIS OF SCENES

MUSICAL NUMBERS

Our Lives Were Different Then
We're The Four Jolly Tars

The music for these songs is given on pages 53–59

Other Farndale Avenue comedies by
David McGillivray and Walter Zerlin Jnr
published by Samuel French Ltd

The Farndale Avenue Housing Estate Townswomen's Guild Dramatic
Society Murder Mystery

The Farndale Avenue Housing Estate Townswomen's Guild Dramatic
Society's Production of *A Christmas Carol*

The Farndale Avenue Housing Estate Townswomen's Guild
Dramatic Society's Production of *Macbeth*

The Haunted Through Lounge and Recessed Dining Nook at Farndale
Castle

They Came from Mars and Landed Outside the Farndale Church
Hall in Time for the Townswomen's Guild's Coffee Morning

The Farndale Avenue Housing Estate
Townswomen's Guild Dramatic Society

A brief history by
Mrs P.J. Reece (Chairman)

The Society was formed in 1932 to cater for a growing need
among ladies in the area who wanted to meet new friends
and do some acting. Our Chairman in those far-off days
was someone whose name escapes me. We have done a great
many plays, both funny and serious, and in 1951 we had
the honour to perform for the Mayor of Guildford although
he was not able to be present. Here are just a few of our
previous productions:

1940	Hindle Wakes
1945	Cavey Girls! It's Miss Wimbush
1947	Doctor Faustus
1949	Brown Owl Knows the Ropes
1956	A Woman's Mission
1958	Hindle Wakes
1959	A Streetcar Named Desire
1963	Larks in the Dingly Dell
1968	Oklahoma!
1972	Now, Now, Your Reverence
1976	Macbeth
1977	Hindle Wakes
1977	Guildford Cavalcade (our contribution to H.M. Queen Elizabeth's silver jubilee).
1978	The Farndale Follies
1979	Hindle Wakes
1980	Murder at Checkmate Manor
1982	Chase Me Up the Garden, s'il vous plait
1984	The Romans in Britain (all female amateur premiere)
1985	Goodnight Mrs Puffin
1986	The Sea Gull
1987	Aida
1988	Double bill: Cheeky Chops the Sausage Dog/ Hindle Wakes
1989	Hindle Wakes

We welcome applications from new members, particularly
those ladies who are interested in backstage work. We
rehearse Mondays, Wednesdays and Fridays from 7-9 p.m.

PROLOGUE

Either behind the house tabs or in view of the audience is a set representing the deck of the SS "Farndale Avenue", a luxury ocean liner. The railing of the ship is upstage. The backcloth shows a beautiful blue sky. In view of the audience, c, is a disc jockey's mixing console

The House Lights are up. If it's an open stage the Lights are to half. If it's a proscenium arch stage there is some light on the apron. In the auditorium the music of Noël Coward is playing

When the audience come in they are greeted by Mrs Reece, Thelma and Felicity, who sell programmes, each of which contains an identical bingo card (see page 45), and one of which bears a red star. The ladies show people to their seats, and apologize for the fact that, due to a double booking, a man arrived earlier and set up disco equipment. Mrs Reece mounts the stage. The Lights come up to full

Mrs Reece Has anyone got the right time? Is that the verdict of you all? No votes for ten to eight?

Thelma I told you so.

Mrs Reece I'm just lagging behind the merest trifle. It's not the end of the world, is it? All right, Thelma. We'd better get started. It's eight o'clock.

Thelma, immobile, looks daggers at Mrs Reece

Come along, dear. I want to get off early tonight. I've got some people coming round.

Thelma I do beg your pardon. I didn't realize. I'll just phone the police and arrange a motor-cycle escort.

Mrs Reece Don't bother, dear. Just send a couple of men on to get rid of this thing, will you?

Thelma exits

That's Mrs Greenwood. For those who haven't had the pleasure. Well, good-evening, ladies and gentlemen, and thank you so much for coming along tonight to see our play. You have all come to see the play, haven't you? There's nobody here for the disco, is there? You are? What—and all you people over here? Oh, dear. This is most unfortunate. Look, I'm sorry. There's not going to be a disco here tonight. I really am sorry. Particularly as you've got dressed up for it. But there's been the most dreadful mix-up. It's nothing to do with us of course. We booked the hall simply ages ago and I told this extraordinary young gentleman in sunglasses that there was no point in setting up his gramophone thing because we're doing a play. But he was so persistent. Felicity, could you do something about this? Thelma's obviously not going to lift a finger.

While Mrs Reece continues speaking, Felicity attempts to drag off the mixing console

So there we have it. If you young people would like to stay and see the play, you're more than welcome. There is some music and dancing in it as a matter of fact. It's not the modern kind of course. But at least it's got a bit of a melody, not like this blessed thump-thump-thump business we have to put up with today. It's not really music, is it ... ?

The DJ enters

DJ Let's get busy! What is this, an encounter group? I want to see you on your feet!
Mrs Reece I thought we'd settled all this ...
DJ (*to Felicity*) Hey! You want those arms to stay in their sockets?
Felicity Are you talking to me?
DJ Don't mess with that gear! *Verstehen Sie?*
Felicity She told me to do it.
Mrs Reece May I just have a quick word?
DJ How are you doing out there? Are you ready to party? Come on, everybody in the house say "yeah"!
Mrs Reece Excuse me.
DJ Can't hear you. One more time! Yeah!
Felicity Yeah!
Mrs Reece Felicity!

The DJ puts on a record. The House Lights go down and flashing disco lights come up on stage

Adrian? What are you playing at up there?
DJ (*through microphone; over the intro to the record*) This is the first of tonight's truly massive killer cuts here at the (*name of theatre*) and when I say "move!" I want to see you get up out of your seat and make your body move!

While the record plays, Mrs Reece attempts to attract the electrician's attention and to stop Felicity jiggling about to the music. Finally she takes the needle off the record

Mrs Reece I really am going to get one of my headaches if you don't stop making this terrible noise.
DJ Lay off the equipment, lady, I'm warning you!

He replaces the needle and the music is heard. Almost immediately Mrs Reece takes the needle off again. The DJ replaces it. These actions continue until Mrs Reece removes the record from the turntable

Mrs Reece Right, you're not having this record back until we've discussed——
DJ Give me that record back.
Mrs Reece Not until we've discussed the matter in hand.

DJ What's to discuss?

Mrs Reece Do you never clean these records? Look at this. It needs a good wipe with a damp Spontex.

DJ Get off my stage!

Mrs Reece It's our stage!

DJ Where's your contract?

Mrs Reece Adrian, have you completely taken leave of your senses?

The disco lighting fades and general lighting comes up

I should think so too.

DJ Show me your contract.

Mrs Reece Would you mind stepping over here, please? Felicity, hold the fort, would you?

While Mrs Reece talks to the DJ, Felicity thinks of what she can do to hold the fort, then begins a tap routine

(*To the DJ*) Now it cannot have escaped your attention that this audience is not in the mood for loud music. And in addition to that, we have several elderly people here with severe back problems so there is no question of them getting on down and making their bodies move and all that sort of malarkey. What's this?

DJ I booked this gig three months ago. That's my contract signed by both parties. Where's yours?

Mrs Reece Felicity. Felicity!

Felicity What?

Mrs Reece Where's our contract?

Felicity What contract?

Mrs Reece It's around here somewhere. I'll get it in a minute.

DJ I paid the rental in advance. That's my receipt.

Mrs Reece Yes. Ours is in the post.

DJ And that's my entertainment licence. You haven't got one of them either, have you?

Mrs Reece Since when do you need a licence to be entertaining? I've never heard such rot.

The DJ takes back his record

DJ Ta.

Mrs Reece Couldn't we come to some kind of arrangement? Why don't we have a cup of tea and a chat? Felicity! Felicity, stop showing off and go and get a couple of teas.

Felicity Now?

Mrs Reece Yes, right now. I'll have half a cup, no sugar.

Felicity exits

Perhaps we could do the play and then you could do the disco afterwards? I might even have a bit of a Twist myself. Or don't they do that any more?

DJ It is time to get funky!

Music blares out again. The flashing lights resume. Mrs Reece shakes her fist at the electrician then stands thinking what to do next

   Felicity enters with a cup of tea

Mrs Reece takes the tea. After a few moments her attention moves to the console then back to her cup of tea. When the DJ isn't looking, she pours the tea into the console. There is a bang, a flash and the music grinds to a halt. The flashing lights fade and general lighting comes up

   Flash Gordon Bennett!
Mrs Reece Was that supposed to happen?
DJ Listen, everybody, there ain't gonna be no show tonight ...
Mrs Reece Oh, rotten luck.
DJ Unless I can get back home and get a replacement.
Mrs Reece You don't think that'll be too tiring?
DJ Couple of hours there and back.
Mrs Reece That long?

Pause. She and Felicity look at each other

   Well, why don't you rush off and get whatever you need and we'll try and
   keep everyone amused until you get back?
DJ You just happen to have something planned, I suppose?
Mrs Reece Well, we're not professionals like you with licences to entertain.
   But I expect we can put on some kind of show. Do you want to do your
   gymnastic display, Felicity?
Felicity I've put my leotard in the wash.
Mrs Reece Well, it doesn't matter. I expect we'll have a sing-song.
DJ I thought you were going to do your crappy play.
Mrs Reece I don't think there's any need for that kind of language.
DJ I don't care what you do. Just don't be here when I get back.
   Comprenez-vous?

   The DJ exits

Felicity resumes the struggle with the mixing console

Mrs Reece *Absolument, monsieur, et merci beaucoup. (To the audience)* Have
   you ever encountered such an odious creature?

   The DJ enters

DJ And don't touch that gear!
Mrs Reece The very idea! No, no. We'll act round it. It's not in the way at
   all.

   The DJ exits

   (To Felicity) There's an empty skip outside the back door.

   With the help of a member of the stage staff, Felicity removes the console

Now where was I? Oh, yes. Good-evening, ladies and gentlemen. My nerves are in tatters. Let's pretend that regrettable incident never occurred. Justice prevailed. That's the main thing. And now we're going to carry on with the play ...

Thelma (*off*) About time!

Mrs Reece But before we do I'd like to remind the ladies that the hand drier in the ladies' toilet is inoperative. Well, it's operative, but it's sucking instead of blowing. And we've already lost two charm bracelets, a finger-stall and half a pound of jelly babies. So if you are going to wash your hands, ladies, please try not to get them wet. I also have to remind everyone here of the resolution passed at last month's AGM regarding dunking. Shall I read it? Just so there are no misunderstandings. "The dunking of biscuits and similar comestibles into hot beverages is offensive to the majority of members and is therefore no longer permissible at any Guild function." So do remember that the entire theatre has been designated a dunk-free zone. And if anyone really cannot resist the urge to have a quick dunk during the interval, would he or she please go to the dunking area? Turn left out of the building, walk two hundred yards——

Thelma (*off*) I'm not waiting much longer, Phoebe!

Mrs Reece On second thoughts, could you get a map from Mrs Wolstenholme? She'll be in the foyer with a side parting and a mole. But now it's time to turn back the clock to an age of glamour, romance and enchantment. Thank you, Adrian.

The Lights fade to Black-out

And don't forget there's bingo after the interval.

Black-out

Mrs Reece exits. Felicity enters as Cicely the 1st Flapper

(*Off*) Would you mind not yelling at me for all to hear?

Thelma (*off*) This is a total and utter fiasco, Phoebe.

Mrs Reece (*off*) It might have helped if you'd applied for a licence.

Thelma (*off*) That's not my business!

Mrs Reece (*off*) Well, it's not mine.

ACT I

The deck of the SS "Farndale Avenue", moored in an English port on a bright summer's day in 1930

The voices of Mrs Reece and Thelma are drowned out by the sound of crowds cheering and a ship's siren

The Lights come up on Cicely waving goodbye to people on the dock below

Cicely Goodbye! Goodbye! Goodbye! Goodbye! (*Etc., ad lib*)

Evidently anxious about being the only person on stage, she eventually wanders off

(*Off*) Where are they?

Black-out

Cicely enters, followed by Gordon as Gwendolyn, the 2nd Flapper

The Lights come up on the Flappers waving

Flappers Goodbye! Goodbye! Goodbye! Goodbye! (*Etc., ad lib*)

Their right arms are aching from waving and they alternate with their left. They sneak glances at their watches

Finally Mrs Reece enters as Lillian the 3rd Flapper and joins the group waving at the railing

Lillian There's never enough time to say goodbye properly.
Cicely There was so much more——
Lillian Sorry. My zip stuck. Carry on.
Cicely There was so much more I wanted to say.

Pause

Gwendolyn Goodbye . . .
Lillian No. (*Prompting Gwendolyn*) Never mind.
Gwendolyn Sorry.
Lillian (*prompting Gwendolyn*) Never mind.
Gwendolyn OK.
Lillian That's your line. Never mind . . .
Gwendolyn Oh. Never mind.
Lillian (*prompting Gwendolyn*) Cicely.
Gwendolyn Cicely.
Lillian (*prompting Gwendolyn*) Never mind, Cicely. We'll write simply screeds and screeds of letters . . .

Gwendolyn (*joining in*) We'll write simply screeds and screeds of letters . . .

Lillian (*prompting Gwendolyn*) When we get . . .

Gwendolyn When we get to Rome.

Lillian (*correcting Gwendolyn incorrectly*) Florence.

Gwendolyn Florence.

Cicely Oh, Naples . . . !

Lillian Naples. Sorry.

Cicely Naples! I just know I'm going to fall devastatingly in love there.

Lillian I think I'm in love already.

Cicely Lillian, what can you mean?

Lillian I mean the captain, silly. Who else? Look surprised, Gordon. I do hope we're dining at his table.

Cicely How dreadfully forward of you, Lillian.

Lillian And how dreadfully forward of you, Cicely, to trip up the gang-plank into the arms of the Chief Petty Officer.

Cicely *Touché*, my dear. But he does have the most delectable beard. Don't you agree, Gwendolyn?

Lillian (*prompting Gwendolyn*) Yes.

Gwendolyn Yes.

Lillian And are you going to tell us which of the crew you find most attractive, Gwendolyn dear? Could it be the stoker?

Gwendolyn Yeah.

Lillian And what is it about him that sets your senses aflame? I expect it's his brawny arms, isn't it?

Gwendolyn Yeah.

Lillian We wormed it out of you, didn't we?

Cicely Oh, isn't it all too devilishly exciting? Do let's go to our cabins and change into something nautical.

Gwendolyn moves off R. *Cicely pulls her back*

Lillian Yes, let's. I'm in number one.

Cicely I'm in number two.

Lillian Take a stab at it, Gordon, for pity's sake.

Gwendolyn I'm in number one.

Lillian *I'm* in number one!

Gwendolyn (*imitating her*) *I'm* in number one!

Lillian All right. We're both in number one. Whoopee! We can have pillow fights.

Cicely gives a little scream of surprise

Scream, Gordon.

Gwendolyn screams hysterically

(*Hitting Gwendolyn to stop her*) Not like that! Give me strength. What is it, girls?

Cicely Look who's coming aboard!

Lillian (*instructing Gwendolyn*) Lean over the rail.

Cicely It's Constance Lombard, the West End stage star.

Part of the rail breaks beneath Gwendolyn's weight

Gordon, you're being an absolute pain.
Gwendolyn I'm not supposed to be Gwendolyn!

Lillian tries to push Gwendolyn's knees together

Lillian People haven't paid to see that, dear.
Cicely Do let's see if——
Lillian Just a moment, Felicity (*To the audience*) I must explain, ladies and
gentlemen: Gordon's just standing in, you see. Sylvia Frobisher was
supposed to be playing this part, but she's got the double glazing men in.
So much for priorities, I hear you cry. Well, I couldn't agree with you
more and I'll be bringing this up at the committee meeting. (*To the
Flappers*) And ever onward, people. What's happening?
Cicely Constance Lombard's coming aboard.
Lillian Oh, yes. Do let's see if we can get her autograph. Off.

She pushes Gwendolyn off

Cicely Do let's see if we can get her autograph. That was my line, Mrs
Reece.

Cicely exits L

*There is the sound of a ship's siren and cheering crowds. Flashes, representing
camera flashbulbs, are seen from the wings. The following taped voices are
heard*

1st Man's Voice Mind if we take some pictures, Miss Lombard?
2nd Man's Voice This way, please, Miss Lombard.
Constance's Voice How do you want me, boys?
1st Man's Voice That's just great.
2nd Man's Voice What's the purpose of your trip, Miss Lombard?
Constance's Voice (*laughing*) That's an easy one. Pleasure!
1st Man's Voice Is it true you're going to Naples to marry Olympic
swimming champion Beauregard St Clair?
Constance's Voice So my secret's out, is it? All right, I admit it, and you can
quote me as saying that I'm the most deliriously happy girl in the world.
2nd Man's Voice Give us that smile again, Miss Lombard.
1st Man's Voice Over here, Miss Lombard.
Constance's Voice You've got all you need boys. I'll see you in a month . . .
or two . . . or three!

Thelma enters L *in wide-brimmed hat and long string of beads as Constance
Lombard*

Constance Sometimes I long for a private life.

Meanwhile, the tape continues

2nd Man's Voice Just one more, Miss Lombard.
Constance's Voice All right, Tom. This one's just for you.

Constance hurriedly exits R

2nd Man's Voice Wow! That's dynamite, Miss Lombard.
1st Man's Voice Is it true you'll be retiring from the stage, Miss Lombard?
Constance's Voice I shall never retire, Joe. And you can print that in capital letters. Now please let me board the SS *Farndale Avenue*. If I miss this ship, I shall never forgive you.
Men's Voices Thanks, Miss Lombard. You're a sport.

Pause

Constance enters R

Constance Sometimes I long for a private life. (*Calling off* R) Bring my luggage up here, Daisy.

Felicity enters L *as Constance's maid Daisy, carrying a pile of boxes. She sees Constance, who indicates she should enter* R

Quickly as you can, girl.

Daisy exits L *and hurries* R *behind the backcloth*

We hear a thump, a cry and a crash of boxes. Constance wanders C

(*Waving*) Goodbye!

Daisy enters R *with dented boxes, fewer than before*

Daisy Cor lummy, it's a climb and a half up that gangplank and no mistake. Where d'you want the stuff, mum?
Constance Take it to my state room, please, Daisy. And treat it with the utmost solicitude. If anything happened to my priceless collection of Capo di Monte porcelain, I would open a vein.
Daisy Bless your heart, mum, I'd sooner strangle me firstborn than let any harm befall your precious *objets d'art*.

She exits L, *dropping boxes* en route *and kicking them into the wings*

Constance Thank you, Daisy. I know I can rely on you.

She is startled by another burst of crowd cheering

Goodbye, everyone! Don't worry, I'm not deserting you. I'll be back in the West End, but as Mrs Beauregard St Clair. Look at those simple, trusting faces. I must accept my destiny as a public figure who is able to give pleasure to common folk.

She exits L, *colliding with Mrs Reece entering as Beauregard St Clair in a smart suit and overcoat*

Beauregard Wrong side, dear.
Constance Doesn't matter.
Beauregard As you wish.

As he enters he (accidentally?) catches Constance's string of beads, which breaks

Bring my luggage up here, porter.

Constance Phoebe! Look what you've done!

Beauregard Take care of it and there's ten shillings in it for you.

Constance bends to retrieve the fallen beads

Constance This is positively the last time I'm lending my valuable property to these productions.

Felicity enters L as a Porter wheeling a trolley bearing one battered box

Porter Right you are, Mr St Clair, sir.

Beauregard You can't come on there, Felicity.

Porter I've always come on here.

Beauregard We've established that the gangplank is over there, haven't we? We've all been looking at it. You can't bring my luggage on from the quoits court. What would it be doing there, I ask you?

Constance You can get your own jewellery from now on.

Beauregard You shouldn't be on, Thelma.

Porter Right you are, Mr St Clair, sir.

The Porter exits L

Beauregard I told you not to address me as Mr St Clair. I don't want anyone to know I'm aboard this ship, especially my fiancée Constance Lombard. Thelma, you're making a mockery of these lines.

Constance I'm not leaving until every bead is accounted for.

The Porter drives his trolley into the backcloth, bringing it down and revealing step-ladders and other theatrical bric-à-brac

Beauregard Are you having some trouble back there, Felicity?

Porter Just bringing your luggage, sir.

Beauregard Yes, my fiancée is under the impression that I'm meeting her in Naples and I'm positive she has no idea I'm so close at hand.

Constance Move your foot.

Beauregard Sorry. I plan to astonish her tonight at the Captain's table. I can't wait to see her expression of pure delight.

Constance, close to Beauregard, gives him a look of pure malevolence before she exits

The ship's siren is heard

Voice (*off*) All ashore that's going ashore!

Beauregard It seems as though we're about to sail.

The Porter enters R with squashed cardboard barely recognizable as a box

Porter Blooming heck! That gangplank fair took the wind out of me, sir. What's in these fine boxes if I might be so bold?

Beauregard Delicate, wafer-thin porcelain from the reign of Queen Anne. It's worth a small fortune.

Porter Present for Miss Lombard, sir? It's well-known how she prizes such costly relics.

Beauregard Correct. Here's a little something for you (*he searches his pockets*) for being so fastidiously attentive. (*He hands the Porter a half-eaten sandwich*)

Porter I shall buy a bottle of champagne with this and drink to your health, Mr St——

Beauregard Careful, my man.

Porter Sorry, sir. Nearly forgot.

The Porter exits L

Beauregard Goodbye! Goodbye!

The orchestra is heard playing the song "Our Lives Were Different Then" (see page 52)

There's an orchestra on the quayside. How enchanting!

Gordon enters R as Noël Nightingale in yachting outfit and sunglasses

This song brings back so many happy memories for me.

Noël Yes. Strange how potent cheap music is.

Beauregard I wish I could remember the title.

Noël Allow me to assist. It's a silly little thing called "Our Different Lives Were Lived Differently ... or something" and I wrote it in nineteen ... twenty ... thing ... for my intimate revue *Bottoms Ahoy*.

Beauregard *Bell* Bottoms Ahoy.

Noël Sorry.

Beauregard Then you must be Noël Nightingale.

Noël At *votre service*.

Beauregard What brings you aboard the SS *Farndale Avenue*?

Noël I'm going to ...

Beauregard N ... n ... n ...

Noël I'm going to Nairobi to ...

Beauregard Naples!

Noël I'm going to Naples to write my latest musical. I shall call it *Neapolitan Nosebag*.

Beauregard It sounds like a winner to me.

Noël Bring my luggage up here, Porter.

Beauregard It's "nosegay", dear, not "nosebag".

Noël What?

The Porter enters shamefacedly carrying a large piece of torn paper, a ribbon and a suitcase handle

Beauregard Doesn't matter.

Porter Is this your luggage, sir?

Noël Yes, the Louis Vuitton trunk and the five snakeskin suitcases are all mine. So is the briefcase in hand-tooled Moroccan leather. Will you pass it to me, please?

The Porter passes Noël the ribbon. He and Beauregard whisper behind Noël's back

Beauregard Go and get the luggage, Felicity!
Porter I can't. It's all bashed-up and squashed and some of it's under the backcloth and I tried to pull it out, but this handle came off. It's a complete mess!
Beauregard But that's Thelma's personal luggage. She's taking it to Marbella next week. I'd better try to explain to her. (*He makes to move off* L)
Thelma (*screaming; off*) Who's responsible for this?

Beauregard returns C

Beauregard It's not an ideal moment. Shall we carry on?
Noël Do you mind of I smoke, Mr... er ... ?
Beauregard St—I mean ... Smith. No, please feel free.

The Porter rolls up his piece of torn paper and hands it to Noël, who puts it in his mouth. The Porter is about to light it for him when Beauregard intervenes

Don't be so silly! He'll have no eyebrows left.
Noël I've got to smoke something, Mrs Reece.

Beauregard produces another dog-eared sandwich

Beauregard The very thing.
Noël What?
Beauregard Smoked salmon.

Noël uses it in lieu of a cigarette

Noël What a beastly chill wind coming off the Channel.
Porter Would you like your overcoat, sir?
Noël Yes, please, Porter. It's in one of my suitcases. No, not that one. That's full of manuscripts. The one next to it. Yes, that's it.

After some hesitation the Porter hands Noël the suitcase handle. Noël considers it, then places it on his shoulder. The music fades up and the Lights fade to Black-out

Everyone exits

The backcloth is replaced. The Lights come up. The music fades out. It is sunset, the same day

After a moment, Constance enters, veiled. She moves C *to the rail. Noël enters and joins her*

Admiring the view?
Constance Yes.

The backcloth crashes down to the ground

I've never seen a sunset quite like that before.
Noël Idyllic, isn't it?
Constance Utterly.

Pause. The next two lines are supposed to be said simultaneously but aren't

Haven't we met ... ?
Noël Forgive me for ...
Both Ha-ha-ha-ha!
Noël After you.
Constance You first.
Noël No, I insist.
Constance Ha-ha-ha-ha!

Pause. The next two lines are supposed to be said simultaneously but aren't

I was just going to say ... Ha-ha-ha-ha!
Noël I was just going to say ... oh, I'm sorry. I interrupted you again.
   (*Prompting her*) Now you laugh.
Constance (*irritably*) I've done it.
Noël Who is it then?
Constance You.
Noël Give us a clue.
Constance I could never forget ...
Noël I could never forget ... I've forgotten.
Constance (*pointedly*) Ha-ha-ha-ha!
Noël I could never forget that malodorous laugh.
Constance Melodious laugh!
Noël That's what I said.
Constance And I could never forget that inimitably well-bred gentility.

Noël scratches his crutch

It's Noël Nightingale, isn't it?
Noël (*removing his sunglasses*) At *votre service*. It's Constance Lombard,
   isn't it?

*Constance attempts to remove her veil, but it is wrapped too tightly round her
face. She claws at the netting with increasing fury and finally tears into the
material and rips it from her face*

Constance The same.
Noël Darling heart.
Constance Precious dreamboy.
Noël Angel delight.

*They embrace. Noël makes several attempts to kiss Constance on the lips, but
she keeps shifting her head away*

Constance Just on the cheek, Gordon. It must have been about a century
   since we were chums at Oxford. Kiss me again, my darling.

She moves away. Noël follows

What brings you aboard the SS *Farndale Avenue*?
Noël Aren't we going to do the other kiss?
Constance Pardon?
Noël I've got this line where I say "Your lips are as irresistible as always"
   and then our mouths meet fleetingly at first but are drawn together again
   as if by a magnetic force.

Constance (*ignoring him*) What brings you aboard the SS *Farndale Avenue*?
Noël Your lips are as irresistible as always.
Constance So we've established. Are you going to tell me what you're doing on this ship or am I supposed to be psychic?
Noël Is it me again?
Constance When you're ready.
Noël I think it's time for a cocktail.
Mrs Reece (*off*) No, it isn't!
Noël Isn't it?

Mrs Reece appears, struggling into a Steward's jacket

Mrs Reece That's page twenty-one. I haven't changed yet.

She exits

Noël Then let's go and play quoits.
Constance Darling Noël, you old scatterbrain. Has it completely slipped your mind that you're on your way to Naples to write another of your captivating musicals?
Noël Didn't I say that?
Constance What's this incipient smash hit to be called?
Noël *Neolithic Gay ... bag.*
Constance How pretty.
Noël It's about a brilliant playwright from good stock who goes abroad to forget about his devastating relationship with a woman from the lower orders.
Constance Not taken from life, I trust?
Noël Alas. She was a fool. I was a maidservant. We were to be wed. But it was quite, quite impossible.
Constance Naturally. You poor dear.
Noël Let's go and play quoits.

Noël exits

Constance Don't you want to know something about me, Noël my angel?
Noël (*off*) No.
Constance I'm going to Naples to marry Beauregard St Clair, you know. Just in case you wondered.

Noël enters

Noël Quoits?
Constance Cocktails!
Noël Yes. Shall we repair to the cocktail lounge?
Constance It's such an enchanting evening. Do let's have our cocktails up here.
Noël A cracking good idea.
Constance I'll call over that aged, hunched steward. I say there, old fellow!

Pause

Are you coming or aren't you?

Mrs Reece, dressed as a Steward, pushes on a covered trolley

Steward Are you talking to me, dear? I never would have realized from that description.

Constance We'll have two cocktails and get on with it.

Steward Certainly, madam. A great favourite with today's bright young things is a Slow Comfortable Rummage in the Church Hall Annexe. For this we dip the rim of a tumbler in lightly-beaten egg white and caster sugar. We stir in a mixture of cracked ice, gin, kirsch, lemon juice and two teaspoons of sugar syrup. Then we top up with soda water and decorate with cherries draped over the rim.

Constance }
Noël   } *(together)* Two of those, please.

Steward Coming right up.

During the ensuing dialogue and song, the Steward uncovers the trolley revealing unsuitable cocktail ingredients such as washing-up liquid, bleach, detergent, pasta shells, cornflakes, HP Sauce and custard powder. He mixes them in a cocktail shaker, pours the brew into cocktail glasses and decorates them with orange slices and umbrellas

Constance Ha-ha-ha-ha-ha!

Noël Has something tickled your fancy?

Constance I was just thinking back to the days when we were penniless students.

Noël Those days of unendurable hardship. By the end of Hilary we could barely scrape together the price of a Fortnum's hamper.

Constance But it was such fun scrimping and saving, wasn't it? I mean I never dreamed I'd take a taxi to lectures, but I said to myself, "Constance, you've just got to rough it", and that's when I paid off the chauffeur. It was so jolly living like an ordinary person.

Noël Did one even have to comb one's own hair?

Constance I believe one did. And do you remember all those other simple pastimes we used to enjoy?

Pause

Steward That's a cue, Joyce.

The orchestra is heard playing a very slow introduction to "Our Lives Were Different Then". It gets faster as an adjustment is made to the speed of the record

Our Lives Were Different Then

Constance	Do you still remember the midsummer fête?
Noël	How we'd wait at the gate
	For we'd hate to miss the raffle.
	Our lives were different then.

Do you still remember the Farndale church hall?

	I'd install a mirror ball.
Constance	I would call the old time dance steps
	Our lives were different then.

Noël	Today I live in style,
	I cruise the Nile and gamble in Vegas.
Constance	My home is just divine.
	With walls of pine and ceilings by Degas.

Both	But we still remember bottling plums,
	Meeting chums, trimming tums:
	All this comes from growing older.
	Our lives were different then.

The orchestra repeats verses 1 and 2 during which Noël ineptly partners Constance in a dance

Constance	Today I own three yachts
	And lots and lots of pure silk pajamas.
Noël	I bought a town in Greece,
	But sold the lease to buy the Bahamas.

Both	But we still recall through rose-tinted haze
	Salad days, flower displays;
	Let us raise our glasses to them:
	Our lives were different then—were different then.

Steward Your cocktails, madam.
Constance Thank you. (*Her lip curls as she looks into her glass*)
Noël Here's to romance.
Constance (*uncertainly*) Romance.

They chink glasses. Noël downs his cocktail in one, then looks queasily at the empty glass. Constance moves UC *to the railing*

Why, look! An albatross.

A badly-made, stuffed white bird is hurled US *of the railing from wings* R *to wings* L

Isn't that supposed to be desperately unlucky?
Steward That's just an old superstition, madam. Nothing to worry about.
Constance Here it comes again.

The bird is flung from L *to* R

It seems to be circling the ship. Almost as if it were trying to warn us of some impending catastrophe.
Steward An albatross you say?

The bird is thrown on from R *and hits the Steward in the face*

I can't see it. (*He throws it into the funnel*)
Constance No, it's flown off now.

Steward Looks like a storm up ahead. Another cocktail, madam?

Constance Let me think. (*She stretches her arm behind a flat and empties her glass*) Yes, why not? And what about you, Noël? Would you like another cocktail?

Noël (*feebly*) Rather.

The Steward pours two more cocktails

Steward I do hope you'll be able to visit our duty-free shop, madam. This week's special offer is an exquisite range of porcelain.

Noël dutifully drinks his cocktail. Constance stares at him in astonishment, then gives him her cocktail, which he also drinks

Constance How delightful.

Steward Dinner will be served at eight. This is tonight's menu. *Bon appetit!*

The Steward exits with the trolley

Constance Well, this looks too scrumptious for words. We'll be starting with truffled goat's liver in aspic and then to follow there's oysters stuffed with curried eggs in a thick mustard sauce, and finally marzipan pastries floating in Belgian chocolate syrup. I do hope they'll be served with wicked dollops of clotted cream.

Noël carefully puts his head inside the funnel and is apparently very ill. He emerges

Noël Let's go and play quoits.

Noël exits L

Constance I'll be along in a trice. I just want to spend a moment thinking about my beloved Beauregard. I feel strangely close to him tonight. (*She hums "Our Lives Were Different Then"*)

Daisy enters upstage of the railing

Daisy Begging your pardon, mum ...

Constance (*sotto voce*) What do you think you're playing at?

Daisy Don't I come on here?

Constance (*sotto voce*) You're in the sea!

Daisy realizes and exits doing the breast stroke with puffed cheeks

Constance continues humming

Daisy enters R

Daisy Begging your pardon, mum, but which of your lovely evening gowns shall I lay out for dinner?

Constance Did we bring the white satin?

Daisy I knew that was your favourite so I popped it in the wash last night. It's come up a treat.

Constance (*prompting her*) You'll be the prettiest and most desirable woman on the ship.

Daisy You'll be the prettiest and most desirable woman on the ship.

Constance Stop it, Daisy. I won't hear another word. If anyone wants me I shall be playing quoits with Mr Nightingale.

Daisy Not Mr Noël Nightingale the playwright?

Constance That's him. He's one of my oldest friends.

Daisy (*aside*) Oh, lummy. That's torn it.

Beauregard enters L *in a dinner-jacket with a glass of liquid*

Beauregard Give that to Gordon. I'm on.

Constance What's this?

Beauregard He's got an upset stomach. Please, Thelma! We're not supposed to meet yet. Hallo there, Daisy . . .

Constance I'm not a waitress, Phoebe.

Beauregard Gordon is being terribly sick over there. If you don't give that to him, he'll miss his next cue. Hallo there, Daisy.

Daisy Mr St Clair . . .

Constance Gordon! Gordon, stop that this instant!

Constance hurries off L

Daisy As I live and breathe! What are you doing here, sir?

Beauregard Keep your voice down, Daisy. I don't want Miss Lombard to know I'm on board.

Daisy You old slyboots, sir. What have you got up your sleeve?

Beauregard A little surprise for later this evening. At the captain's table I shall present her with a fabulously expensive porcelain figurine.

Constance enters L *holding up a white satin evening gown covered in vomit*

Daisy She'll be thrilled to bits, sir. Oh! and you wait till you see her. She'll be looking like a princess in the most dazzling and seductive sheer white satin evening gown ever created for a woman.

Her voice tails off as she and Beauregard see Constance

Constance I'd like to speak to you, Phoebe.

Beauregard (*innocently*) What about, dear?

Constance Apparently Gordon told you he was going to be sick and you said, "Don't do it here. Do it over that old bit of satin curtain material."

Beauregard As if I'd say a thing like that!

Constance Tonight you have systematically destroyed some of my most treasured possessions.

Beauregard Do bear with us, ladies and gentlemen.

Constance My jewellery——

Beauregard That was an accident——

Constance What about my luggage?

Beauregard Let's talk about this later.

Constance We'll talk about it now. This is a Balmain original!

Beauregard It just needs soaking overnight. In the meantime we can get you something out of the Oxfam sack. Felicity, go to the boiler-room and get——

Constance Right, I've had about as much as I can stand of this. I'm going home.

Beauregard Oh, not all this again.

Constance Not all what again?

Beauregard Thelma, you have threatened to walk out of every play we have produced for the past twenty years.

Constance That is a gross distortion of the truth.

Beauregard You were going to walk out of *Julius Caesar* because Mrs Gilbert stabbed you too hard.

Constance She was using a real knife!

Beauregard You were going to walk out of *Peter Pan*.

Constance I suffered concussion in that play, Phoebe.

Beauregard You should have checked that the window was open before you flew out of it.

Constance I'm an actress, not a scene-shifter!

Daisy She was going to walk out of *Cat On a Hot Tin Roof*——

Constance I'm not standing here while you run through my curriculum vitae——

Beauregard Well, why don't you go if you're going?

Daisy (*querulously*) Mrs Reece, no!

Constance Right! I will! (*She marches off the stage and through the auditorium. To an audience member*) What are you staring at?

Constance leaves the auditorium

Beauregard Where were we?

Daisy We can't carry on without Thelma.

Beauregard She'll be back in ... (*he consults his watch*) ... five minutes, thirty-two seconds. Your line I think.

Daisy You'll have to forgive me, sir. I've got to go and lay out the mistress's evening gown.

Beauregard You run along then, my girl.

Daisy While I think of it, sir, is it true that Mr Noël Nightingale's on board?

Beauregard Yes, I met him earlier. He seems like a decent enough cove.

Daisy I shouldn't speak out of turn, sir, but you don't know him like what I does. We was engaged to be wed.

Daisy exits R, crying

Beauregard Well, I'll be blowed.

Noël enters L, looking ill, in dinner-jacket

Evening, Nightingale old man. You look a picture of health.

Noël Thanks, Smith. I must say I feel on top of the world. I've just been playing ... some game or other ... with that devilishly attractive ... whatever her name is.

Beauregard You know her?

Noël Intimately. I had a bit of a pash on her at Oxford and now I do believe I'm ... going to be ...

Beauregard You're falling in love with her all over again?

Noël Is there anywhere I can lie down?

Beauregard Make an effort, Gordon, please.

Noël Are you dining at the captain's table tonight?

Beauregard Of course.

Noël Then I'll introduce you.

Beauregard That's uncommonly civil of you, old man. I believe the captain has promised that tonight we can dine under the stars. Isn't that so, Captain?

Jones (*off*) Indeed it is.

Felicity enters as the bearded Captain Jones, but has not managed to change completely out of Daisy's costume. He carries with him a picnic table, which he erects DR *and during the ensuing scene continues to bring more items on to the stage*

Good-evening, gentlemen. I am Captain Jones.

Beauregard Bring a chair.

Jones I'm going to. It's my pleasure to be able to welcome you to my table tonight.

Jones brings on four camping chairs

Noël collapses into the first of them

Beauregard Very kind of you to invite us. I must say I'm particularly looking forward to the truffled goat's liver. Will you be serving it *à la provençale*? That's the wrong chair, Gordon. Come and sit over here.

Jones Will Miss Lombard be joining us?

Beauregard Yes, any minute.

Jones Are you sure?

Beauregard Just bring those other chairs in, Felicity.

Thunder and lightning

Oh dear, I do hope we're not going to get tossed about. (*To Gordon*) On second thoughts we'll have you back where you were. Upsy-daisy. It seems we're in for a bit of a squall. Get your head off the table, Gordon. There's such a thing as etiquette, you know.

Noël Where's the toilet?

Jones The old *Farndale Avenue* is the sturdiest vessel in the fleet, sir.

Beauregard How comforting.

Jones Aperitif?

Beauregard Not for me, thank you.

Noël I'll have another of those delicious cocktails.

Jones Certainly, sir.

Jones goes off and brings on a cocktail shaker and glasses

He pours another emetic brew, which Noël drinks through gritted teeth

Beauregard I hear that after dinner there's to be an international floor show and dancing to two orchestras.

Noël I can't wait to fling myself round the dance floor.

Beauregard I can't wait to meet Miss Lombard.
Noël You don't have to, Smith, Here she comes.
Jones What are we going to do, Mrs Reece?
Beauregard Ssshh! (*Consulting his watch*) Five, four, three, two, one.

Thunder and lightning

> *The auditorium door bursts open and Constance strides down the aisle and on to the stage wearing an unsuitable red dress*

Constance For the sake of my friends who've paid good money to see me, I shall finish tonight's performance, but this will be my last appearance with this Society.
Beauregard We'd better make the most of it then, dear.
Constance For your information I've been headhunted by the [*local amateur dramatic society*].
Beauregard Fancy.
Constance They want me to play the lead in *Beauty and the Beast*.
Beauregard I shan't ask the obvious question.
Constance (*to Noël*) What are you staring at?
Noël Is the circus in town?
Beauregard He's not well. Constance, my darling! Surprise, surprise.
Constance Beauregard! What are you doing here?

> *Jones fetches an electric candelabra with a cable running into the wings. He holds a lighted match over the bulbs and waits for the electrician to connect the power. The candelabra finally lights*

Beauregard I couldn't bear to be away from you, my angel, so I booked the same passage to Naples.
Constance Beauregard, you shouldn't have.
Noël You know each other?
Constance Of course. This is my fiancé, Beauregard St. Clair, the Olympic swimming champion.
Beauregard Sorry, Nightingale old man. I had to preserve my anonymity.
Noël You must think I'm an utter cad and a bounder.
Beauregard Nonsense, old man.
Jones Hors d'oeuvres.
Constance Oh, super. I'm famished.

During the ensuing conversation, Jones crowds the table with crockery, cutlery and plates of cold porridge dyed various colours, which continues to upset Noël's constitution

Beauregard A little present for you, my dearest.
Constance Is it ... is it ... ? (*She opens a box and takes out an unrecognizable, battered lump*) It is.
Beauregard Is it what you wanted, darling?
Constance You know how I adore the intricate craftsmanship of Queen Anne porcelain.
Jones I can glue the other bits on to it, Thelma. You'll never know, really.

Noël I've got a present for you as well.
Constance Oh, do let me see.
Noël I've forgotten it.

Jones rushes off

It's just coming.
Constance Be still my heart.
Beauregard Eat up, Gordon.

Jones enters with an object hastily wrapped in newspaper

Noël I got it at the duty free.

Constance unwraps a bottle of washing-up liquid

Constance I'm overwhelmed.
Jones Now you'll have an exquisite set of porcelain figurines, madam.
Constance (*pushing the presents on to Jones*) I shall treasure them.
Jones May I serve the main course?
Noël No ... no ... no ...
Beauregard (*scraping his food on to Noël's plate*) A large portion for me,
  Captain, if you please.
Jones You haven't finished yours, Thelma.
Constance I'm not eating it. It's disgusting.
Jones You've got to. You're famished.
Constance Don't tell me what I've got to do.
Noël You're looking very lovely you know, in this damned moonlight,
  Constance.

Moonlight suddenly snaps on

Constance Moonlight is cruelly deceptive.
Beauregard What did you say, Constance?
Constance We were discussing the moonlight, my darling.
Beauregard There's nothing between you and this Nightingale fellow, is
  there?
Constance Of course not, Beauregard. We're just old chums from Oxford.
Noël What did you say, Constance?
Constance I'm trying to pacify Beauregard. He's being insanely jealous. I
  expect he's only here to spy on me.
Jones Sweet!
Beauregard (*scraping his food on to Noël's plate*) I'm ready.
Jones Thelma, you haven't even started your hors-d'oeuvre yet.
Constance I'm not eating it!
Jones Just try some of this. It's really nice.
Constance I'm warning you.
Jones I know you're hungry. Would you like some of this with it?

Constance stabs Jones's hand with a fork

Ow! Mrs Reece! I've been stabbed!

Beauregard This is supposed to be a romantic comedy. It's turning into Grand Guignol.
Jones It's bleeding!

Beauregard throws her a napkin

Beauregard Don't bleed over the table. Do I hear a waltz?

Raucous pop music is heard briefly then stops. Thirties' waltz music plays

Constance The dancing has begun. Which of you gentlemen will partner me?

Noël appears to be about to throw up in Beauregard's lap

Beauregard I think Noël's particularly eager, dear. Can you help me rush him to the dance floor?

Constance and Beauregard attempt to carry Noël off. He tries to make a detour via the funnel and is pulled away from it towards the wings

Quickly as you can, dear, or we'll all be sorry.
Noël Lovely meal, Captain.
Beauregard Carry on, Felicity.

Constance, Beauregard and Noël exit

Much thunder and lightning. Black-out. Jones is lit only by the candelabra

Jones It's all right, ladies and gentlemen, the emergency lighting will be on in a minute. And you have my word that the good old SS *Farndale Avenue* will weather this dreadful storm and that very soon we'll all be in sunny Napoli. But right now it's my pleasure to be able to tell you that it's showtime here on the SS *Farndale Avenue* and that for the next two hours we'll be bringing you a galaxy of your favourite entertainers beginning with The Four Jolly Tars!

Shouts from off that The Four Jolly Tars are not ready

But before we see The Four Jolly Tars let me remind you of some of the rest of tonight's entertainers. In just a moment Mrs Evans will be giving a talk on the nuthatch and other tree-creeping birds, with slides. Then Mr Solomons will be here to tell us about diseases in the golden hamster. As a special treat we've managed to persuade Mrs Rollett to come along and read Chapter One of another of her unpublished books. This one's called "A Girl's Childhood in Basildon".

Shouts from off that The Four Jolly Tars are ready

But right now will you please welcome those saucy sailors, those merry matelots, The Four Jolly Tars.

The candelabra goes out. The backcloth is replaced

Jones exits. Mrs Reece (1), Thelma (2) and Gordon (3) enter in white sailor suits as The Four Jolly Tars

There is colourful lighting as the trio sing and perform hornpipe routines

We're The Four Jolly Tars

All	We're The Four Jolly Tars
	And we sail the seas
	In a sweet little vessel
	Called the *Ocean Breeze*.
1	I'm number one.
2	I'm number two.
3	I'm number three, that's who.
All	And while we wait for number four we'll do a dance for you.

Yes, we'll wait for number four and do a dance for you,
Yes, we'll wait for number four and do a dance for you,
Well, the score's not four,
And we need one more,
So we'll wait for number four and do a dance for you.

Dance

	We're The Four Jolly Tars
	And we all drink rum tots,
	And we like to sing shanties
	While we're tying our knots.
1	I'm number one,
2	I'm number two,
3	I'm number three, my dears.
All	And we'll do another dance until the fourth appears,

Yes, we'll do another dance until the fourth appears,
Yes, we'll do another dance until the fourth appears,
We need another one
To make it much more fun,
So we'll do another dance until the fourth appears.

Another dance during which Felicity (4) joins the others in a bloodstained sailor suit, carrying an anchor

	We're The Four Jolly Tars
1 and 2	And we're present:
3 and 4	Correct!
All	But we're leaving very shortly
	'Cause the ship gets wrecked.
1	I'm number one,
2	I'm number two,
3	I'm number three,
4	I'm number four.
All	You'd better make the most of this, you won't get more.

Yes, you'd better make the most of this, you won't get more,
Yes, you'd better make the most of this, you won't get more,

There's a great big crash,
And we all go splash,
So you'd better make the most of this, you won't get more.

As a finale to the number, the Lights dim and the anchor is illuminated. The Lights are restored to full. There is a tremendous crash. The Lights flicker. Everybody screams

Thelma What's happening?
Felicity I'll go and see.

She runs to the rail. A bucket of water is thrown in her face

It's nothing to worry about, ladies and gentlemen, but the ship's sinking.

Dramatic music. Hysteria and running about

Man the lifeboats!
Mrs Reece Townswomen and children first!

Gordon tries to remove the lifebelt from the rail and fails. In his struggle he removes the entire rail and puts it round his head. The women run backwards and forwards carrying "important" items, e.g. anything amusing and bizarre found in the theatre. The Lights fade to Black-out. A spot comes up C on a model representing the ship sinking beneath the waves. After it disappears, a squirt of water, as from a soda syphon, shoots up. Black-out

Everyone exits

The House Lights come up

ENTR'ACTE

C *is a tombola (with numbered balls inside) and a table with a rack for the selected balls*

The Lights come up as Mrs Reece mounts the stage

Mrs Reece (*reproachfully pointing out members of the audience*) This lady down here with (*description*). Gentleman over there with (*description*). Yes, you. And the lady at the back with (*description*) looking very sheepish as well you might. What are you? Dunkers. It's not funny. And don't protest. Because you were seen in the act. I'm sorry, in my day it was known as letting the side down. I'll say no more. Now last week the Guild Committee chose the winner of our competition to find a new name for the church hall in Farndale Avenue, and they thought it would be a bit grand if I announced the results tonight. So that's what I'm going to do. They're in this sealed envelope here and now I'm going to reveal all. Well, the winner of the competition is Mrs Parry Jones—congratulations!—and now let's see what the hall's going to be called. Oh, isn't that lovely? It's going to be called "The Farndale Avenue Church Hall". I think that's rather appropriate, don't you? Good. Now if you've all got your bingo cards ready—have you got them? They're on the back page of the programme, you can't miss them. So if my glamorous assistant would care to join me, we can get our eyes down. Where's my glamorous assistant?

Thelma enters wearing something stunning

Can you send on my glamorous assistant, Thelma? Just a little joke, dear. Do you know what you're doing? I'll hand you a ball and you put it in the rack, but do make sure the number on the ball is the same as the number on the rack . . .

Thelma I'm not sub-normal, Phoebe.

Mrs Reece That's what I keep telling everyone, dear. All right, folk, remember we're playing for a really super prize tonight so as soon as you've crossed out every number on your card, shout out something terribly loudly at me. What can you shout? "I think I'm the winner" . . .

Thelma Bingo.

Mrs Reece What?

Thelma They don't say "I think I'm the winner", they say "bingo".

Mrs Reece All right, dear. Apparently the winner has to say "I think I'm the bingo". I'm not very up on these technical terms. Shall we rehearse that?

Thelma We don't need a rehearsal!

Mrs Reece Better safe than sorry, I always say.

Thelma I thought you wanted to get off early tonight.

Mrs Reece I'm just about to start.

Thelma Well, get a move on.

Mrs Reece All right. Don't blame me if it all goes wrong. Stand by for your first number. And it's lucky for some—forty-seven. All the commandments—number ten. All the disciples plus seven—nineteen. My age—sweet sixteen.

Thelma Wait a minute. (*She turns the ball the other way round*) Phoebe's age—sweet ninety-one.

Mrs Reece Membership of Thelma's fan club—one. Seven and six. Was she worth it? I've never understood what that meant, but still. Two little ducks—fifty-five. The number of minutes to roast a leg of lamb—sixty-nine. That's at gas mark two, mind. Lucky for some—twenty-four. My husband's inside leg measurement—thirty-two.

Since all the bingo cards are identical, everyone with a programme will now shout out

No, only one person calls out. You see? I knew they hadn't got the hang of it, Thelma.

Thelma (*calling into the wings*) Who did the bingo cards?

Felicity enters

Felicity I did.

Thelma You're supposed to make some of them different.

Felicity Mrs Reece said it didn't matter.

Mrs Reece Thank you, Felicity. Would you mind clearing away these things, please?

Thelma And bring on about a hundred and twenty prizes.

Mrs Reece That won't be necessary, Thelma, because I have averted the crisis.

Felicity clears the tombola and table into the wings then exits

Ladies and gentlemen, in readiness for tonight's raffle, which we had to cancel because there are at present twenty-six raffle tickets inside the hand drier in the ladies' toilet, there is somewhere in the hall tonight, a programme with a lucky red star on it. And we're going to give tonight's super bingo prize to whoever's got it.

Mrs Reece chats ad lib about where to look for the red star, then encourages the winner out of his or her seat and reminds him or her to bring the programme

Thelma shows the winner on to the stage then exits

Hallo! What's your name? Can I have a look at your programme? I hate having to check up, but people can't be relied on like the old days. Do you see that man over there? He gave us his solemn word he wouldn't have a dunk in the interval. Mrs Wolstenholme caught him in the vestibule with his hand up to his wrist. Poor Mrs W. We had to sedate her. Anyway, this is quite in order. Here's the star. So allow me to present you with your prize: it's your very own model of a luxury liner, which you can put together yourself, but do be careful with that glue, won't you, because you read so many strange stories. Congratulations!

The winner leaves the stage

And now, aided by the magic of the theatre, let's travel to the bottom of the sea and find out what's going on there.

The Lights and House Lights fade to Black-out

Mrs Reece exits

ACT II

Underwater

Nautical music and ultra-violet light

During the ensuing "underwater" sequence the cast, in black costumes, gloves and masks, carry fluorescent-painted hardboard cut-outs of the ship, fish, knives and forks, etc., which glow in the UV light

A shoal of fish swims past, then a duck

The SS "Farndale Avenue" appears high above the playing area (perhaps on a stick) and sinks to stage level before disappearing

An octopus moves quickly across the stage, carried by two people. The tentacles are detached from the body, and the octopus leaves the stage in two halves

Four plaice appear and a cruet shakes salt and pepper over them. The plaice vanish, reappearing in a circular design, which spins while knives and forks move in and out from the circle. Everything vanishes

The four plaice return. A shark appears and swallows the plaice. Moments later the shark's jaws open and a line of skeletons swims out. Shark and skeletons disappear

A sign reading "Sea bed" appears. A larger version of the ship appears from the wings and floats diagonally to the stage. A patchwork quilt is pulled over it

The music finishes and snoring is heard. Black-out

Everyone exits

SCENE 2

A desert island

The same backcloth can be used. There is also a palm tree, some sand, the wreckage of the SS "Farndale Avenue" and DR is a barrel

Noël enters in a white suit with polo-neck jumper, rolled-up trouser legs, a cravat and a straw hat

Noël   How perfectly horrid;
                      This island's deserted.
                      The temperature's torrid;
                      My ship is inverted.

Hmmmm. Scratches his head and sits on barrel. (*He does so*) Perhaps I
could use that for the second act of my musical.

*A three-dimensional white grand piano painted on a piece of hardboard is
pushed on from the wings. Piano music is heard (a setting of Noël's first four
lines). Noël mimes playing the piano and sings a completely different tune*

                      How perfectly horrid;
                      This island's deserted.
                      The temperature's torrid;
                      My ship is inverted.
                      No! It's imposs——

*Three loud dischords as if the keys have been struck in anger. Noël swings his
hands back to the keyboard too violently and knocks the piano over*

(*Speaking*) No! It's impossibly dismal. And yet how well it matches my
gloom as I languish alone on this godforsaken island.

*The piano plays the intro to "Our Lives Were Different Then". Noël sings
along*

                      Do you still remember how we would swear

Beauregard enters with his suit tattered in standard castaway style

Beauregard   That we'd share
                      Our Tupperware?
                      What a pair ...

*Simultaneously, the piano music grinds to a halt and there is a Black-out.
Beauregard's voice fades away*

Well, that's got Act Two off on the right foot. Adrian!
Adrian (*off, or from lighting box*) Sorry, Mrs Reece. Something's gone
wrong.
Beauregard Yes, I rather gathered that. Will you be able to lighten our
darkness, dear?

The Lights come up

Hallelujah. And can we have the piano music back on as well? (*To the
audience*) Not that Noël isn't really playing the piano, I hasten to add.
This is just a technical thing. I don't even understand it myself.
Adrian (*off*) I can't play this bit of tape, Mrs Reece. Someone left a mug of
tea on the control board and it's gone over everything.
Beauregard Who would do a stupid thing like that? I'm sorry, I'm going to
speak my mind now: people who spill tea over sound equipment are
irresponsible. Don't you agree, Gordon?

Adrian (*off*) Mrs Reece, is your tea mug the one with "Phoebe is the greatest" on it?

Beauregard Yes, why?

Adrian (*off*) That's the one that got spilled.

Beauregard (*abruptly*) We needn't bother with the song. Are my eyes deceiving me?

Noël Nightingale.

Beauregard That's you.

Noël St Clair!

Beauregard Nightingale!

Noël Ha-ha-ha-ha!

Beauregard Ha-ha!

Noël Fancy seeing you here.

Beauregard I'm an Olympic swimming champion.

Noël Yes, I know.

Beauregard So it's just the two of us.

Noël No. I'm here on my own.

Beauregard I see. It's very hot out here.

Noël Yes, it is.

Beauregard How did you escape from the shipwreck?

Noël I clung to the grand piano. And you?

Beauregard I'm an Olympic swimming champion.

Noël Ah.

Beauregard So here we are.

Noël Fancy seeing you here.

Beauregard Ha-ha!

Noël Ha-ha-ha-ha!

Beauregard It's very hot out here.

Noël Yes, there's no air conditioning.

Beauregard Is there anyone else on the island?

Noël Yes. It's just the two of us.

Beauregard Ha-ha!

Noël Ha-ha-ha-ha!

Beauregard How did you say you escaped from the shipwreck?

Noël I clung to the grand piano.

Beauregard I remember now.

Noël And you?

Beauregard Well, it's funny you should ask that because . . . I'm an Olympic swimming champion.

Noël Fancy seeing you here.

Beauregard Well, it's certainly hot.

Noël I expect it's the sun.

Beauregard Possibly. Ha-ha!

Noël Ha-ha-ha-ha!

Beauregard Is there anything else you'd like to tell me about the island?

Noël I got here by clinging to the——

Beauregard We're in no doubt as to your mode of transport.

Noël There's an oak tree over there.

Beauregard It's a palm tree.
Noël There's a plum tree over there.
Beauregard P-a-l-m!
Noël There's a ... plam tree over there ...
Beauregard Is it really just the two of us alone on this island?
Noël Yes, it's really just the two of us.
Beauregard What about the woman we both loved?
Noël Who's that?
Beauregard Constance.
Noël Oh! Yes, Constance is here.
Beauregard No she's not.
Noël That's right. I shall never survive.
Beauregard Yes, we shall, with the aid of this book, *How to Survive on a Desert Island.* It was written by Mrs Clarke-Benson, who was stranded on Ibiza when her plane was delayed for three hours. Let's see now ...

Noël rummages beneath the palm tree

Ah! Here we are: how to make a nutritious meal. First pick two coconuts.

Noël produces two items nothing like coconuts. During the remainder of the recipe he finds other unsuitable objects

These will be used as mixing bowls. How resourceful! Then gather together the root of the jacaranda tree, half a pound of seaweed, a small swordfish, the hoof of a giraffe ...
Noël That's a tall order.
Beauregard Ha-ha-ha!
Noël Fancy seeing you here.
Beauregard Don't start that again! We mix well and simmer for two to three hours, but to save time, we've got one we prepared earlier.

Noël presents Beauregard with a doughnut covered in cream

I wonder if it's as tasty as it looks?
Noël Let's see.

After taking successive bites, he has the whole doughnut in his mouth

Beauregard Come on, Noël, out with it.

Noël makes unsuccessful attempts to speak while spitting out doughnut

Spit it out, Noël.

Noël chews and swallows every morsel of the doughnut, a prolonged piece of comic business, which should take sixty-five seconds minimum

Noël (*finally*) Yum yum.
Beauregard Shall we go and explore the island?
Noël I might need the toilet again.

They move to exit R

Daisy enters R. *Her maid's uniform is in tatters, and her hand is wrapped in a bloody bandage. She produces occasional spurts of blood by pressing a bulb leading to a tube hidden under her costume*

Daisy I can't stop it bleeding, Mrs Reece.
Beauregard This isn't casualty, Felicity.

He and Noël exit R

Daisy Let's rest under this palm tree, mum. It was a long crawl up the beach.

Constance enters in white sarong, carrying a parasol

Constance Where are we, Daisy?
Daisy Well, it ain't the Old Kent Road, mum.
Constance Daisy, what's to become of me? I'm stranded here in the middle of nowhere and nobody knows where I am.
Daisy Perk up, mum. At least we made it safely from the ship to this island thanks to them passing dolphins.
Constance Did they bring the luggage as well?
Daisy Yes, mum.
Constance And the porcelain?
Daisy Yes, everything, mum. Except ...
Constance Except what?
Daisy One of the little blighters dropped the travelling iron.
Constance What? You stupid animals! Can't you do anything properly? Oh! Now what am I going to do? I'm going to look like a tramp.
Daisy Don't worry yourself, mum. I'll work out a way of pressing your lovely frocks between two boulders.
Constance Dear Daisy. What would I do without you? Oh! What's this pinned to the tree? A piece of paper.
Daisy Oh, God. (*She searches the stage for something to use as a piece of paper*)
Constance What on earth is a piece of paper doing pinned to this tree?
Daisy I meant to set it. I meant to. I'm not well, Thelma. Look.
Constance Take it away from me. Just get the paper.

In desperation Daisy lugs the piano over to the tree

Daisy I've got it right here, mum, and stone the crows if it ain't a piece of paper just like what you said. Cor! Blooming heck.
Constance There seems to be some writing on it.
Daisy It's a blinking map, that's what it is right enough. What shall we do with it?
Constance I'll fold it up and put it ... (*she indicates that she was supposed to place it in her cleavage*) ... where no harm shall come to it.

Daisy attempts to hand her the piano. Constance moves away

And now I shall lie down here in this crumpled sarong and try to sleep. Will you put your arms round me like you did when I was a little girl?
Daisy Of course I will, mum.

Constance Don't you dare touch me!

A fountain of blood sprays over Constance's costume

Get away from me!

Daisy I can't help it, Thelma.

Constance Go over there!

Daisy We've got to stay here.

Constance Right, I'll go over there then. (*She moves away from Daisy*) Oh, Daisy, I feel so safe and secure in your arms. I don't think anything could ever frighten me again.

A ridiculously large tarantula descends slowly from the flies. Constance opens half an eye and realizes that she is now lying in the wrong position to be menaced by it. She tries to shift herself surreptitiously so that her face is lying directly in the spider's path. The spider almost reaches Constance and then seems to jam

Oh, come on, come on! (*She reaches up, pulls the spider on to her face and then screams*)

Noël and Beauregard enter R

Noël That scream came from this direction.

Beauregard My God! Look!

Noël It's Constance.

Dramatic music. While Daisy sits watching, Noël fights with the spider. First he struggles to remove it from Constance's face. He succeeds, but it goes for him instead. Constance gets up. Beauregard comes to Noël's assistance and it goes for Beauregard. Noël pulls it off and swings it across the stage. Constance ducks to avoid it. Noël catches it again and he and Beauregard try to control it, pulling it down to C *and then stamping on it when it is on the floor. The music stops*

It's all right now. It's dead.

Constance Oh, Noël!

Music. The spider is pulled up again. Beauregard pats it over to Constance. She pulls it towards her and struggles with it. Daisy gets up to help. Constance doesn't see her and elbows her in the face, knocking her to the ground again. Noël pulls the spider off Constance, but overbalances and collides with Beauregard, who suffers a minor injury. Noël is distracted, leaving the spider to dangle. Constance pretends the spider is still attacking her then tugs at the rope, bringing it down. She throws the rope and spider into the wings. The music stops

Darling Noël! You came back to save me.

Noël (*to Beauregard*) Are you all right?

Constance (*pulling Noël to her*) I thought you were dead.

Noël (*looking for the spider*) It won't hurt you any more, Miss Lombard.

Constance I've done all that. Nice to see you again, too, Beauregard.

Beauregard Just thinking of you made me swim all the faster, my love.

Constance How touching.

Noël I think a celebration is called for. I say, Daisy, any chance of rustling up some lapsang souchong with lemon?

Daisy (*with blood coming from her mouth*) I'm ever so sorry, sir, but as I was going down for the third time, I only managed to grab the powdered milk.

Noël Poor show, Daisy.

Constance There's worse. We've lost the travelling iron.

Beauregard Never mind. With the aid of this book, I can build a house.

Daisy I can collect sticks to make a fire.

Constance I can do my hair.

Noël And I can play the piano.

Beauregard That's the spirit.

Beauregard and Daisy exit

Noël (*sitting at the piano*) What would you like to hear?

Constance Something romantic.

Noël Do you remember this?

He vamps the intro to "We're The Four Jolly Tars". This time, however, the instrument heard is a church organ

Constance How could I forget? It's that dear little sailor song they were playing on the ship the night we ... we ...

Noël Fell in love all over again?

Constance Don't say that, my darling.

Noël gets up from the piano. The music continues for a short period

Noël You know it's true.

Constance Yes, it's true.

Noël Beloved enchantress. You drive me wild with desire. I think I'm going to be sick again.

Constance (*passionately*) You so much as dribble on this sarong and I'll wring your neck. Kiss me, adorable Romeo.

Another thwarted kiss

On the cheek, thank you. Oh, what, mad, mad rapture! But I'm engaged to be married to Beauregard.

Noël You must tell him your heart belongs to another.

Constance Of course. Why didn't I think of that? Play for me, my darling. I want to abandon myself in a dance of desire.

Noël mimes playing "We're The Three Jolly Tars", presented in several styles to give Constance the opportunity to show her versatility as a dancer

At one point she is joined by a chorus consisting of Mrs Reece and Felicity dressed as a lobster and a crab respectively

Noël You dance like Stanley Matthews.

Constance Jessie Matthews!

Noël Sorry.

Constance It's you who inspire me, my darling.

Noël Shall we go for a dip?

Constance You go ahead and bag a couple of sun-loungers before the Germans get here. I'll find my beach ball.

Noël exits

I'll find my beach ball. Where can it be? I'll find my beach ball!

Mrs Reece pokes her head round a flat

Beauregard I'm perfectly well aware of what the cue is. I just can't get out of the lobster, that's all.

Constance Just get on here!

After a little more struggling Mrs Reece walks on in the character of Beauregard, but dressed as the lobster

Beauregard Ah! there you are, Constance.

Constance Hallo, Beauregard.

Beauregard Golly, it's hot working in this sun. You don't think I'm getting too red, do you?

Constance I really wouldn't know.

Beauregard I've finished building the house. Would you like to come and design the cushion covers?

Constance Sorry, Beauregard. I'm just off for a swim with Noël.

Beauregard You've been bewitched by this philanderer. Do I have to shake some sense into you?

There is no contact between them

Constance Stop it, let go of me, you're hurting me! Beauregard! You're behaving like an animal!

Beauregard He doesn't love you. I do.

Constance You just want to get me into your claws. Well, I shan't let you. I'm going to him!

Constance runs off. Daisy enters, dropping firewood and staggering weakly to the barrel

Beauregard Can you manage, dear?

Daisy (*nodding*) I've lost quite a bit of blood though.

Beauregard (*surveying the blood-spattered stage*) It's not lost, dear. We know exactly where it is. I suppose you heard that ghastly row, Daisy.

Daisy Seems we've both been jilted, sir.

Beauregard Where did I go wrong? Could I have been more attentive? Am I too short? Should I have wooed her with a fifty-piece orchestra? Do you think we could start again? Is there any chance?

Daisy Yes, sir.

Beauregard Yes, there's a chance?

Daisy Yes, you're too short, sir.

Beauregard By Jove, your down-to-earth humour cheers me up no end, Daisy. This Nightingale fellow, was he a monstrous beast to you?

Daisy It wasn't his fault, sir. We was from different worlds, like. I tried to better myself. (*With cut-glass accent*) "Lord love a duck, guv," I says to him, "I could talk posh like what you does and no geezer would smell a rat nohow." (*Resuming Cockney*) But Mr Nightingale said it would never work. "Cor blimey," I says to him, "what more do you want from me, blood?"

Beauregard You poor creature. Have you tried Dettol, dear?

Noël and Constance enter

Constance I've been playing catch with Noël but we had to stop because he got one of his balls stuck in a sand dune.

Noël I say! What's this in the sand? A piece of paper!

He pulls out a hot-water bottle. Beauregard secretes it again

Beauregard Easy mistake to make, Noël, but I understand that this is actually the piece of paper to which you're referring.

Constance It's the one I told you about, Noël. It must have slipped down my garment.

Beauregard Is there anything on it?

Noël (*to Beauregard*) Is there?

Beauregard Yes, it's a map showing the location of buried treasure.

Noël Yes, it's a trap showing the burial of collated pressure.

Beauregard Oh!

Constance Oh!

Daisy groans

On this island?

Beauregard (*prompting Noël*) Yes.

Noël Yes.

Constance How do we find it?

Beauregard A shadow will point the way during the next solar eclipse.

Noël What she said.

Constance What a coincidence! Here comes an eclipse of the sun right now.

Black-out

I'm so frightened.

Noël I'm here, beloved.

Beauregard Nothing can harm you, Constance.

Daisy Mrs Reece, I don't feel very well.

Beauregard Deep breaths, dear.

Noël Look! The light is returning.

The Lights fade up

Beauregard What an awe-inspiring natural phenomenon.

A (black cloth) shadow of the palm tree runs across the stage from the base of the tree to either the edge of the stage or the playing area

Constance Could that be the shadow mentioned on the map?

Noël Is it?
Beauregard Yes.
Noël Yes, it is.
Beauregard (*prompting Noël*) We've got to take ...
Noël We've got to take.
Beauregard (*prompting Noël*) Twenty paces ...
Noël We've got to take twenty paces.
Beauregard (*prompting Noël*) Along the shadow!

| **Noël** We've got to take twenty paces along the shadow. One, two, three, four, five, six, seven, eight, nine, ten, eleven, twelve, thirteen, fourteen, fifteen, sixteen seventeen, eighteen, nineteen, twenty. | **Beauregard** Well, do it then! Don't just stand there saying, "We've got to take twenty paces along the shadow." I do despair some- times, Gordon. |

Realizing that he is about to run out of room, Noël finishes by counting very quickly and taking small steps

Beauregard By Jove! The shadow leads right up to the mouth of that cave.
Constance One of us will have to explore it.
Beauregard Well, I can't do any bending because of my back.
Constance And I've just done my hair.
Noël And I can't go ... but I can't remember why.
Daisy I'll go.
Others Hurrah! Good for you, Daisy! What a sport! (*etc.*)

The Lights fade slowly to Black-out

Constance Are you all right in there, Daisy?
Daisy It's a bit dark, mum.
Constance Is it light enough to find the treasure?
Daisy Well, there's something here, mum. I ain't sure what it is. Cripes, now I can see: boxes and boxes of priceless porcelain. What a turn-up for the book.
Constance Can you see any figurines, Daisy? Daisy, give me your answer, do.
Daisy Yes, mum. There's a lovely model of a Viennese townswoman selling jam at a home-produce stall, and ...

There is a crash and Daisy breaks off with a scream

Beauregard Adrian! Could you oblige us, dear?

The Lights come up. Daisy lies slumped beneath the fallen palm tree. There are also cardboard boxes, marked "porcelain", on stage

Beauregard helps Daisy off

Constance Look at all this porcelain Daisy retrieved from the cave. It must be worth a fortune.

Noël Yes, we're probably the richest people in the world.

Constance A fat lot of use that is when we're trapped on this damned island. We're never going to escape, you know. We're all doomed. My public will desert me and I'm going to die alone and forgotten. I think I'm going mad, Noël. I'm going to die! I'm going to die!

Noël No, you're not.

Constance Thank you, Noël. I needed to be brought down to earth. Say you'll always be here when I need you.

Noël Why don't we make it official?

Constance You mean . . .?

Noël Yes. Will you . . . Will you . . . ?

Constance I will!

Black-out

Everyone exits

Hawaiian music. The Lights come up

Beauregard and Noël enter together

Noël Are you sure Daisy is qualified to conduct the service for my wedding to Constance?

Beauregard Yes, she's a lay preacher with the Church of the Sacred Jumble.

Noël If we ever get back to England, you must look us up.

Beauregard Where do you live?

Noël I have a little *pomme de terre* in Guildford.

Beauregard Very flat, Guildford.

Noël I'm just across from the Teasmade showroom. Do you know it?

Beauregard It doesn't look like a Tupperware box, does it? I've always felt that it might.

Noël I say, St Clair, you're not bitter about losing Constance, are you?

Beauregard Of course not. The best man won, old man. Here comes the bride.

Noël goes to the piano and mimes playing to Mendelssohn's "Wedding March"

Constance enters supporting the enfeebled Daisy, who pumps blood over Constance's white wedding dress. Daisy is now wearing a bandage round her head. Blood trickles down her face. Constance dumps Daisy in a pile of sand

Constance The day that every woman dreams of has dawned.

Daisy (*weakly*) Dearly beloved, we are gathered together here in the sight of God, and in the face of this congregation . . .

Constance, Noël and Beauregard crouch down beside Daisy in order to hear her. Constance nudges her

. . . to join together this Man and this Woman in holy Matrimony . . . and I now pronounce you Man and Wife . . .

Constance Not yet! You've missed out the bit about showing just cause ...
Daisy The bit about showing just cause ...
Constance If any man can show just cause why we may not lawfully be joined together, let him now speak. (*Pointedly*) Do you want to say anything, Phoebe?
Beauregard Sorry. I was miles away. Yes, I object. I mean, no, I don't object. Someone over there objects and I'll just go and get her.

Beauregard exits

Daisy I pronounce you Man and Wife ...
Constance Not yet! I think someone's going to object. I just have that feeling. I think someone's going to object any second now. It's very hot out here, isn't it?
Noël It's the sun.
Constance Shut up. Someone had better object soon or I won't be responsible for my actions!
Mrs Reece (*off*) I'm not quite ready, Thelma.
Constance I'll count three. One ... two ... three.

Mrs Reece, as Mavis, enters. She is still dressed in the lobster costume but has managed to don an extravagant hat

Mavis I object to this marriage taking place.
Constance Oh, really? The lobster objects, does he?
Mavis I'm not a lobster, Thelma, as well you know.
Constance You look unnaturally like a lobster to me.
Mavis I am Mavis Smith and I am married to Noël Nightingale.
Constance (*to the audience*) Does anyone believe a word of this?

Noël puts his hand up

No, I didn't think so. There's no point in going any further with this, Phoebe.
Mavis There's only another couple of minutes, dear.
Constance Before I walk off this stage for the last time, I want you to know that you've succeeded, Phoebe. You've broken my spirit. I stand before you a broken woman.
Mavis I'm sure you are, dear, but we must get on. I am Mavis Smith. Gordon! Put your hand down and look surprised.
Constance There comes a time when self-respect simply will not allow any further degradation. And as I look at you, dressed like something that has escaped from an aquarium in a French bistro, I know that time has come.
Mavis Thelma, you're upsetting yourself over nothing. I shouldn't think anyone's even noticed I'm wearing a lobster costume.
Constance I'm going to my dressing-room now. I want to draft a letter to the *Guild Monthly* announcing my retirement from the stage.
Noël You're not going to be in any more plays?
Mavis Of course she is. She's just had her mask fitted for *The Phantom of the Opera.*
Constance I'm withdrawing from public life, Gordon. Of course I'll miss the

lights and the applause, but sooner or later we must all make way for younger actresses, mustn't we? People like dear, dear Felicity, whose youthful vigour is such an inspiration to us all.

Hearing her name, Daisy stumbles to her feet and during the ensuing dialogue wanders aimlessly round the stage, knocking over everything standing

Felicity, you are the future. Soon I will be but a memory. Farewell!

Constance exits

Mavis I'm afraid Mrs Greenwood's been overworking lately. She was rehearsing for *The Phantom* earlier today and by the time we'd got her down from the chandelier she'd missed her elevenses.

Constance enters

Constance I'll just collect my things if you don't mind.
Mavis We've nearly finished, Thelma. This is the last page. I am Mavis Smith and I am married to Noël Nightingale.

Constance begins removing a box of porcelain. She removes from it some broken pieces, rounds on Daisy and hits her

Noël But I thought you were dead.
Mavis No, I was shipwrecked here fifteen years ago.
Constance I'll be sending in a bill for this porcelain.
Mavis You may kiss me if you wish, Noël.
Noël No thanks.
Mavis What?
Noël I can't kiss you. You're a man.
Mavis Don't be a chump, Gordon. I'm a woman now.
Noël But you're Beauregard.
Mavis Do you have to take the palm tree, Thelma?
Constance My husband made it.
Mavis I'm not Beauregard, Gordon! I'm Mavis Smith. Do pay attention. Reunited at last!

Constance takes off Mavis's hat

Constance That's mine as well.
Mavis Don't be so juvenile.
Constance And so's the lobster costume.
Mavis Be my guest! Take it off me!
Constance Put it on a train tomorrow morning. You can send it Red Star, can't you?

Constance exits

Noël Oh, look! What's that on the horizon?

He points at Daisy staggering along next to the backcloth

Mavis I think it's a ship.
Noël We're saved! We're saved!

Mavis Hurrah! I'll climb the palm tree and light a beacon. On second thoughts, why don't I just run down to the beach and wave a hankie?

Mavis exits

Noël This calls for another celebration, Daisy. Get me a cup of mango pulp and be quick about it, girl.

Daisy collapses into the backcloth, bringing it down on top of her

Don't give me any of that lip, young lady.

Daisy moans something inaudible

What? But that changes everything. How do you know that?

Daisy mumbles

Now it all makes sense. I never dreamed that you had another identity. Can you ever forgive me, your Royal Highness?
Brown (*off*) Ahoy there!
Noël Here we are! We're over here!

The prow of a ship is pushed on L

Climbing a step-ladder behind it, Mrs Reece appears "on board" as Captain Brown in a Napoleonic hat and holding a telescope to his eye

Brown Allow me to present myself. I am William Brown, Captain of HMS *Indesit*. Can I be of any assistance, sir?
Daisy Yes. Get an ambulance.

Constance enters R

Brown Can you telephone for an ambulance, Thelma?
Constance That boat's mine as well.
Brown We only need it for another moment, dear.
Constance It's the back wall of our garden shed. I'm taking it home.

Constance exits L

Brown Perhaps you would allow me to escort you back to England, sir?

The prow slides back into the wings revealing Brown standing on the step-ladder

Thelma, that is not funny. This time you've gone too far.

Brown descends the ladder and exits

Noël Three cheers for Captain Brown, everyone! Hip hip hooray! Hip hip hooray! Hip hip hooray!

While Noël is cheering, the prow slides on and off stage several times. We hear a slap followed by a scream

The prow reappears and so does Brown on board

Brown All aboard, me hearties!

Music: "Anchors Aweigh". A precarious-looking gangplank is lowered from the ship. When it reaches the ground, the gangplank and the ship's porthole are illuminated. Streamers and balloons descend from the flies as Noël walks on board. The music finishes

Anchors aweigh!

The DJ enters R

DJ OK, groovers, when I say "move!" I want to see you get up out of your seat and make your body move!

Black-out and simultaneous burst of the record the DJ played at the beginning of the play

CURTAIN

FURNITURE AND PROPERTY LIST

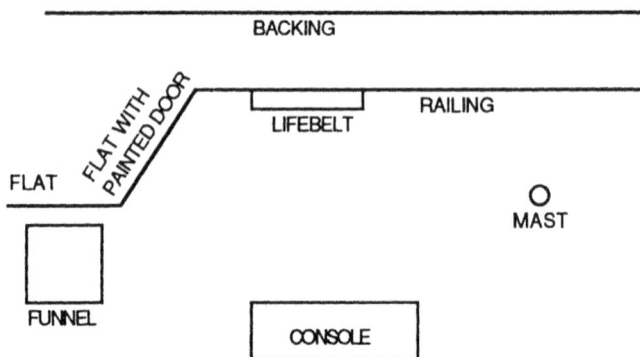

PROLOGUE

On stage: Railing
         Lifebelt
         Funnel
         Disc jockey's mixing console with disco record and microphone (*practical*)

Off stage: Cup of tea **(Felicity)**

Personal: **Thelma, Felicity**: programmes with bingo cards (*one with a red star*), wrist-
         watches (worn throughout)
         Mrs Reece: handbag containing sheet of paper, programmes with bingo
         cards, wrist watch (worn throughout)

Bingo card

1 0				5 5		
		3 2				
						7 6
1 9					6 9	

ACT I

Set: Step-ladders etc. behind backcloth

Off stage: Pile of boxes **(Daisy)**
Four dented boxes **(Daisy)**
Trolley with battered box **(Porter)**
Squashed cardboard **(Porter)**
Large piece of torn paper, ribbon, suitcase handle **(Porter)**
Covered trolley. *On it:* menu card, pasta shells, cornflakes, HP Sauce, custard powder, cocktail shaker, cocktail glasses, orange slices, cocktail umbrellas, bottles of washing-up liquid, bleach and detergent **(Steward)**
Stuffed white bird **(Stage Management)**
Glass of liquid **(Beauregard)**
White satin evening gown covered in vomit **(Constance)**
Picnic table **(Jones)**
4 camping chairs **(Jones)**
Cocktail shaker containing liquid, glasses **(Jones)**
Electric candelabra with cable (*practical*), lighted match **(Jones)**
Crockery, cutlery, plates of cold porridge in various colours, napkins **(Jones)**
Bottle of washing-up liquid hastily wrapped in newspaper **(Jones)**
Anchor **(Jolly Tar 4)**

Personal: **Gwendolyn**: wrist-watch
Constance: string of beads
Beauregard: 2 half-eaten sandwiches in pocket, battered cardboard lump
Noël: sunglasses
Porter: box of matches

ENTR'ACTE

On stage: Tombola with numbered balls inside
          Table. *On it:* rack for the tombola balls, boxed model kit of a ship (for
          prize)

ACT II

On stage: Nil

Off stage: Fluorescent-painted hardboard cut-outs of a shoal of fish; a duck; the SS
          "Farndale Avenue"; an octopus in two halves; four plaice, cruet,
          circular plaice design; "Sea bed" sign; patchwork quilt; shark, line of
          fish skeletons, larger version of the ship **(Cast members)**

ACT II

Scene 2

BACKING

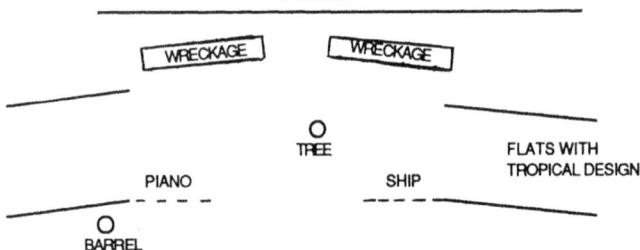

On stage: Sand
          Palm tree. *Beneath it:* various items including cream doughnut
          Barrel

Off stage: White grand piano cut-out **(Stage Management)**
          Large tarantula **(Stage Management)**
          Firewood **(Daisy)**
          Black cloth of palm tree for shadow **(Stage Management)**

During Black-out on page 38

Set: Cardboard boxes marked "porcelain" containing broken pieces of china

Off stage: Ship's prow cut-out with gangplank attached **(Stage Management)**
          Step-ladder **(Captain Brown)**
          Streamers and balloons **(Stage Management)**

Personal: **Beauregard**: book
          Daisy: blood sac attached to tube and bulb, 2nd blood sac
          Constance: parasol
          Noël: hot-water bottle
          Captain Brown: telescope

LIGHTING PLOT

Property fittings required: nil

PROLOGUE

To open: Downstage area lit, house lights on

Cue 1	**Mrs Reece** mounts the stage *Bring up full general lighting*	(Page 1)
Cue 2	**DJ** puts on a record *House lights down, cut to flashing disco lighting*	(Page 2)
Cue 3	**Mrs Reece**: . . . taken leave of your senses?" *Fade disco lighting, bring up full general lighting*	(Page 3)
Cue 4	**DJ**: "It is time to get funky!" *Crossfade to flashing disco lighting*	(Page 4)
Cue 5	There is a bang, a flash and the music grinds to a halt *Cut flashing disco lighting, bring up general lighting*	(Page 4)
Cue 6	**Mrs Reece**: "Thank you, Adrian" *Fade to Black-out*	(Page 5)

ACT I

To open: Full general lighting

Cue 7	**Cicely** (*off*) "Where are they?" *Black-out. When ready, bring up full general lighting*	(Page 6)
Cue 8	The sound of a ship's siren and cheering crowds *Photo-flash effects from the wings*	(Page 8)
Cue 9	The music fades up *Fade to Black-out. When ready, bring up sunset effect*	(Page 12)
Cue 10	**Beauregard**: "Just bring in those other chairs, Felicity." *Lightning*	(Page 20)
Cue 11	**Beauregard**: "Five, four, three, two, one." *Lightning*	(Page 21)
Cue 12	**Jones** waits for the electrician to connect the power *Snap on candelabra*	(Page 21)
Cue 13	**Noël**: ". . . in this damned moonlight, Constance." *Snap off sunset effect, snap on moonlight effect*	(Page 22)
Cue 14	**Constance, Beauregard** and **Noël** exit *Lightning. Black-out, leaving candelabra on*	(Page 23)

Cue 15   **Jones**: "... The four Jolly Tars."   (Page 23)
            Snap off candelabra. When ready, bring up colourful lighting

Cue 16   Finale to "We're The Four Jolly Tars"   (Page 25)
            Dim lighting overall; anchor lights up, then restore full lighting

Cue 17   Tremendous crash   (Page 25)
            Lights flicker

Cue 18   The women run backwards and forwards   (Page 25)
            Fade to Black-out. Bring up spot C *on model ship*

Cue 19   When model ship disappears   (Page 25)
            Black-out

Cue 20   Everyone exits   (Page 25)
            Bring up house lights

ENTR'ACTE

To open: Full general lighting

Cue 21   **Mrs Reece**: "... what's going on there."   (Page 28)
            Fade to Black-out

ACT II SCENE 1

To open: Ultra-violet light

Cue 22   Music finishes and snoring is heard   (Page 29)
            Black-out

ACT II SCENE 2

To open: Full general lighting

Cue 23   **Beauregard** (singing): "What a pair ..."   (Page 30)
            Black-out

Cue 24   **Beauregard**: "... lighten our darkness, dear?"   (Page 30)
            Full general lighting

Cue 25   **Constance**: "... an eclipse of the sun right now."   (Page 37)
            Black-out

Cue 26   **Noël**: "The light is returning."   (Page 37)
            Fade up to full general lighting

Cue 27   **Others**: "What a sport!" (etc.)   (Page 38)
            Slow fade to Black-out

Cue 28   **Beauregard**: "Could you oblige us, dear?"   (Page 38)
            Bring up full general lighting

Cue 29   **Constance**: "I will!"   (Page 39)
            Black-out. When ready, bring up general lighting

Cue 30   When gangplank reaches the ground   (Page 43)
            Dim lighting overall; gangplank and ship's porthole lights up

Cue 31   **DJ**: "... and make your body move!"   (Page 43)
            Black-out

EFFECTS PLOT

Please read the note on page v concerning the use of copyright works

PROLOGUE

Cue 1	To open	(Page 1)
	Music of Noël Coward plays; cut when ready	
Cue 2	**Mrs Reece** pours tea into the console	(Page 4)
	Bang and flash from the console	

ACT I

Cue 3	To open	(Page 6)
	Cheering crowd and ship's siren; cut when ready	
Cue 4	**Cicely** exits L	(Page 8)
	Ship's siren, cheering crowd, taped voices as script pp 8–9	
Cue 5	**Daisy** hurries R behind the backcloth	(Page 9)
	Thump, crash of boxes	
Cue 6	**Constance**: "I know I can rely on you."	(Page 9)
	Burst of crowd cheering	
Cue 7	**Constance** exits R	(Page 10)
	Ship's siren	
Cue 8	**Beauregard**: "Goodbye! Goodbye!"	(Page 11)
	Recording of orchestra playing "Our Lives Were Different Then"	
Cue 9	**Noël** puts the suitcase handle on his shoulder	(Page 12)
	Music fades up	
Cue 10	The Lights come up	(Page 12)
	Fade music	
Cue 11	**Steward**: "That's a cue, Joyce."	(Page 15)
	Recording of orchestra playing very slow introduction to "Our Lives Were Different Then", gradually increasing in speed	
Cue 12	**Beauregard**: "Just bring those other chairs in, Felicity."	(Page 20)
	Thunder	
Cue 13	**Beauregard**: "Five, four, three, two, one."	(Page 21)
	Thunder	
Cue 14	**Beauregard**: "Do I hear a waltz?"	(Page 23)
	Raucous pop music briefly heard, then thirties' waltz music	
Cue 15	**Constance, Beauregard** and **Noël** exit	(Page 23)
	Thunder	

Cue 16	**Jones**: "... The Four Jolly Tars." *Music for "The Four Jolly Tars"*	(Page 23)
Cue 17	The Lights are restored to full *Tremendous crash*	(Page 25)
Cue 18	**Felicity**: "... but the ship's sinking." *Dramatic music*	(Page 25)

ENTR'ACTE

No cues

ACT II

Cue 19	To open *Nautical music*	(Page 29)
Cue 19	As SCENE 1 ends *Music finishes, sound of snoring*	(Page 29)
Cue 21	White grand piano cut-out is pushed on from the wings *Piano music as script p. 30*	(Page 30)
Cue 22	**Beauregard** (singing): "What a pair ..." *Piano music grinds to a halt*	(Page 30)
Cue 23	**Noël**: "It's Constance." *Dramatic music*	(Page 34)
Cue 24	**Noël** and **Beauregard** stamp on the spider *Cut music*	(Page 34)
Cue 25	**Constance**: "Oh, Noël!" *Dramatic music*	(Page 34)
Cue 26	**Constance** throws the rope and spider into the wings *Cut music*	(Page 34)
Cue 27	**Noël**: "Do you remember this?" *Intro vamp to "We're 'The Four Jolly Tars" played on a church organ*	(Page 35)
Cue 28	**Noël** gets up from the piano *Pause, then cut church organ*	(Page 35)
Cue 29	**Constance**: "... in a dance of desire." *"We're The Four Jolly Tars" played in several styles*	(Page 35)
Cue 30	**Daisy**: "... at a home-produce stall and ..." *Crash*	(Page 38)
Cue 31	Everyone exits *Hawaiian music; cut when ready*	(Page 39)
Cue 32	**Noël** goes to the piano and mimes playing *Mendelssohn's "Wedding March"*	(Page 39)
Cue 33	The prow slides on and off stage several times *Slap*	(Page 42)

Cue 34 **Brown**: "All aboard, me hearties!"   (Page 43)
           Music: "Anchors Aweigh"

Cue 35 **DJ**: "... and make your body move!"   (Page 43)
           Burst of disco record played in the Prologue

Our Lives Were Different Then

Do you still remember the midsummer fête?
How we'd wait at the gate
For we'd hate to miss the raffle.
Our lives were different then.

Do you still remember the Farndale church hall?
I'd install a mirror ball.
I would call the old time dance steps.
Our lives were different then.

Today I live in style,
I cruise the Nile and gamble in Vegas.
My home is just divine.
With walls of pine and ceilings by Degas.

But we still remember bottling plums,
Meeting chums, trimming tums:
All this comes from growing older.
Our lives were different then.

Today I own three yachts
And lots and lots of pure silk pajamas.
I bought a town in Greece,
But sold the lease to buy the Bahamas.

But we still recall through rose-tinted haze
Salad days, flower displays;
Let us raise our glasses to them:
Our lives were different then—were different then.

"Our Lives Were Different Then!"

Intro.
Dainty Waltz.

Piano.

Vamp.

Verse.

Voice. 1. Do you still re-mem – ber the mid – sum – mer fete? How we'd wait
2. Do you etc.

Piano. a tempo.

at the gate, for we'd hate to miss the raf – fle, our lives ———

were dif - fer - ent then ———————!

dif - fer - ent then ——————! 1. To - day, I live ———— in
2. To - day, etc.

Chorus.

style ————, I cruise the Nile and gam - ble in Ve - gas; My

home is just di - vine ————, with walls of pine and

rall.

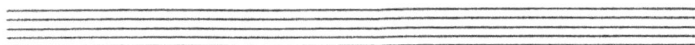

ceil - ings by De - gas! — ha - mas!

D.C. al 🟡

D.C. al 🟡

🟡 Coda.

dif - er - ent then ————————————————, were dif - fer - ent

molto. rall.

then ——————————————!

We're The Four Jolly Tars

We're The Four Jolly Tars,
And we sail the seas
In a sweet little vessel
Called the *Ocean Breeze*.
I'm number one,
I'm number two,
I'm number three, that's who.
And while we wait for number four we'll do a dance for you.

Yes, we'll wait for number four and do a dance for you,
Yes, we'll wait for number four and do a dance for you,
Well, the score's not four,
And we need one more,
So we'll wait for number four and do a dance for you.

We're The Four Jolly Tars,
And we all drink rum tots,
And we like to sing shanties
While we're tying our knots.
I'm number one,
I'm number two,
I'm number three, my dears.
And we'll do another dance until the fourth appears.

Yes we'll do another dance until the fourth appears,
Yes, we'll do another dance until the fourth appears,
We need another one,
To make it much more fun,
So we'll do another dance until the fourth appears.

We're The Four Jolly Tars,
And we're present;
Correct!
But we're leaving very shortly
'Cause the ship gets wrecked.
I'm number one,
I'm number two,
I'm number three,
I'm number four.
You'd better make the most of this, you won't get more.

Yes, you'd better make the most of this, you won't get more,
Yes, you'd better make the most of this, you won't get more,
There's a great big crash,
And we all go splash,
So you'd better make the most of this, you won't get more.

"We're The Four Jolly Tars!"

Voice: We're the Four Jol — ly Tars and we sail the seas, in a sweet lit — tle ves — — sel call'd the "O — cean Breeze." I'm num — ber one; I'm num — ber two; I'm num — ber three, that's who! and while we wait for num-ber four, we'll do a dance for you. Yes! we'll

wait for num-ber four, and do a dance for you! Yes! we'll

wait for num-ber four and do a dance for you. Well! the score's not four and we

need one more, so we'll wait for num-ber four and do a dance for you!

who. you'd bet-ter make the most of this; you won't get more. Yes! you'd

bet-ter make the most of this; you won't get more! There's a great big crash, & we

all go "splash!" so you'd bet-ter make the most of this, you won't get more!

www.ingramcontent.com/pod-product-compliance
Lightning Source LLC
LaVergne TN
LVHW051803080426

835511LV00018B/3394